Learning to Hear God

A PERSONAL RETREAT GUIDE

Learning to Hear God

JAN JOHNSON

NAVPRESS

NAVPRESS⬤

NavPress is the publishing ministry of The Navigators, an international
Christian organization and leader in personal spiritual development.
NavPress is committed to helping people grow spiritually and enjoy lives
of meaning and hope through personal and group resources that are
biblically rooted, culturally relevant, and highly practical.

For a free catalog go to www.NavPress.com
or call 1.800.366.7788 in the United States or 1.800.839.4769 in Canada.

ISBN-13: 978-1-60006-660-3

Cover design by Arvid Wallen
Cover image by Shutterstock

Some of the anecdotal illustrations in this book are true to life and are included with the
permission of the persons involved. All other illustrations are composites of real situations, and any resemblance to people living or dead is coincidental.

Unless otherwise identified, all Scripture quotations in this publication are taken from
the *Holy Bible, New International Version*® (NIV®). Copyright © 1973, 1978, 1984 by
International Bible Society. Used by permission of Zondervan. All rights reserved. Other
versions used include: *THE MESSAGE* (MSG). Copyright © 1993, 1994, 1995, 1996,
2000, 2001, 2002. Used by permission of NavPress Publishing Group; the New Revised
Standard Version (NRSV), copyright © 1989, by the Division of Christian Education
of the National Council of the Churches of Christ in the USA, used by permission, all
rights reserved; the King James Version (KJV); and the New King James Version (NKJV).
Copyright © 1982 by Thomas Nelson, Inc. Used by permission. All rights reserved.

Printed in the United States of America

1 2 3 4 5 6 7 8 / 13 12 11 10 09

Contents

If you have time for only three conversations, you might wish to choose those with * (or you might be led to choose otherwise).

Why Retreat? Making Space for God

I n an age when daily life and even vacations, tours, and cruises are characterized by pressure-packed schedules, a day of retreat invites us to soul-nurturing rest. Jesus said, "I will give you rest," and he is eager to do that (see Matthew 11:28). A retreat as extended Sabbath renews us as we experience solitude and play at a slower rhythm, allowing God more space to interact with us.

Christians throughout the ages have retreated just as Jesus frequently retreated (see Matthew 4:1-11; 14:13,23; 17:1-9; 26:36-46; Mark 6:31; Luke 5:16; 6:12). The format now used of spending the night away from home was begun by very busy Christian workers (those industrious Jesuits) who needed to pause and reflect on their lives. Sometimes their retreats consisted of a day or two; other times, thirty days or more.

Retreat is an attitude as much as a specific event and place. Once you're practiced at it, even a morning in the park can be a retreat. You learn to set aside worries that you'll be bored or lonely. You let yourself be intrigued by the amazing interaction with God in ways you don't expect; you let yourself be calmed by rest that you've needed for a long time.

What a Retreat Is Not

A retreat is not work. It is a sacred space for rest and reflection. Your goal is not to *cover* Bible passages. Instead, by entering deeply into just a few of them, you'll interact with God about how they speak into your life. Your goal is not to come home and feel that you have *achieved* anything. This retreat is not about what you can *do*. It's about interacting with God gently and knowing more about God's true self. Do you believe that God loves you just for your own self, or do you have to be *doing* something to be loved?

The point of this retreat is to help you build a relationship with God. A relationship involves regular personal interaction, ongoing connection, and shared life experiences. You will experience more deeply (yet also gently) what it means to have a life "in God" or "in Christ," as Paul liked to put it.

A retreat is not a nonstop Bible study. Scripture is used as a vital point of contact with God in order to have real conversations with God in each session. This process is based on what is called *lectio divina*, a way that people have prayerfully read the Bible for centuries. Today people often use self-directed effort to apply the Bible to themselves as if to correct themselves through their own strength. In this retreat, come to the Word to be "taught by the Spirit" (1 Corinthians 2:13), which may or may not be correction but just something we need to know. This sort of dialogue is essential to life in Christ.

In these conversations, the Holy Spirit will mentor you by "ask[ing] you questions you hadn't thought of, challenging you to think in new ways, dropping a few gems to capture your imagination, and allowing you to try on a few ideas before guiding you to the true nature of the issue at hand."[1] Expect to be drawn in by the Holy Spirit so that you may not at times be able to "tell where God's words leave off and your intuitive thoughts begin."[2] Now and then, you'll be tempted to launch off onto a tangent, which is sometimes a good idea but other times a distraction from your conversation with God. If you're the kind of person who usually goes off on tangents, resist for a moment and continue focusing on what's in front of you. See what happens. If you don't usually go off on tangents but you get the urge to now, go with it.

Bring a journal of some kind—a spiral notebook or any booklet will do—on your retreat in case you need to write beyond the space provided. Writing in this guide or in a journal isn't something for you to do or complete; it's a way for you to dialogue with God in a concrete way. Don't *try* to journal; just write what goes through your mind.

Don't expect to come home a different person. You probably will be, but not in the ways you notice at first. In fact, you may notice a shift within yourself only after you've been home a few days. But don't look for it. Let God show you what you need to know.

Don't take a retreat because it sounds like a trendy spiritual thing to do. Do it only because you're drawn to do so. Pay attention to the inner nudge. You may be drawn by weariness. You may be drawn by a longing to be with God. You may be drawn for reasons you don't completely understand. If you're doing a retreat only because someone told you that you should, that may create resentment and detract from your experience.

A so-called successful retreat occurs when we keep our "expectations low and the activities quite simple. When we expect our [retreat] to be highly 'spiritual,' it becomes one more thing to do, continuing the addiction to productivity that is so common in our culture."[3]

How Long?

If you'd like to take a personal retreat but you're not sure how to do it, begin by spending a morning in the park once a week for several weeks. Get used to that until you love it and long for more. You can use this guide, one session per week. When you're ready for an overnight retreat, plan for it to be too short rather than too long (but at least twenty-four hours). Leave wishing you could stay longer. Then you'll be ready to come back.

If you want to use this guide for a one-day retreat, you'll need only three sessions at the most. Choose from the seven sessions listed in the contents section, perhaps the ones with the asterisk (*) by them. Choose the ones that most appeal to you.

If you're taking a longer retreat, complete only two or three sessions a day unless you are refreshed and ready to dig in. You will not interact with God well in the sessions unless you have allowed sufficient space to "be" and are well rested. So don't rush, but don't become bored. In general, meeting with God in the morning, afternoon, and evening will be about right. But if you are tired, skip the afternoon one and take a nap or skip the evening one and sit on the porch instead.

If you have time to complete all seven sessions, feel free to skip some and repeat ones in which you sense God particularly speaking to you. In fact, "repetitions" (repeating a session) are a common retreat practice, and the second experience of a session is often better than the first.

The sessions will not be study sessions but times of conversation with God. Feel free to stop to write or think whenever you need to. Try not to let a session last more than ninety minutes. If you're tired, you may find that as little as thirty to forty-five minutes wears you out. See what works best for you.

If you're drawn to a passage other than the ones provided, pause and ask yourself why. Is anything driving you to this passage other than God's direction? (For example, you have to teach on that passage or write an assignment on it.) If you sense that it is specifically God leading you, go ahead and immerse yourself in it in a meditative way.

As you move through the session, feel free to innovate and do things not suggested in the guide. You'll notice that at times you're asked to read the passage slowly. You're on retreat, so you can afford to move slowly and read slowly. Let the words settle within you. At times, you'll be asked to read the passage aloud. Let the words fall on your ears so that you are hearing them as if for the first time. These are the words of your Beloved to you. Cherish each word. Taste and see that God is good.

Space is provided in this guide for you to write your answers. One reason for this is that you will think more clearly if you write things down instead of just muddling through them in your mind. Another reason is that you can then revisit your retreat after you've been home for a while.

In Between Sessions

Begin your day slowly and move slowly all day. Even if you hike or walk, do that slowly. Eat your breakfast slowly. Live by the clock as little as possible. Breathe deeply and take in every color, sound, and texture around you.

After your first session, listen to what's going on inside you. You might need to:

- Take a nap.
- Do something active, such as taking a walk, hiking, swimming, or doing relaxing exercises.
- Just sit and stare. Try "porch sitting," in which you sit and think about nothing in particular. Find a spot to view birds and trees, if possible, and supply yourself with something to drink and a blank pad of paper. You don't have to write anything, but if you wish to, be ready. Or you may wish to sit in a Jacuzzi.
- Do something creative. You might wish to bring art materials (or even a book of art reproductions to look at), a musical instrument, binoculars to watch birds, or perhaps materials needed for you to work with your hands (woodworking, needlework, beadwork). Regarding such work with your hands:

You must not try to get anything accomplished and you don't want it to be mentally taxing (because your mind must be free to rest and linger on what you might be hearing from God). You are doing the activity for fun.

- Do light, meditative reading. You might bring favorite magazine articles that have helped you in the past or books through which God has spoken to you. Read again the underlined parts. Don't bring a detective novel or something that will engage you wholly.

- Use worship music, but remember to enjoy a lot of silence.

Because you are letting your mind rest, these in-between moments will provide space to "connect the dots" from what you lack to what you need. Ideas will coalesce and you'll be surprised at what comes to you. The downtime will create space for you to hear God.

Develop a rhythm for your day(s) that includes rest, prayer periods, time to sit and stare, play (walking, hiking, working with your hands, looking at an art book; avoid video games). Rest a great deal. Look deeply at everything around you. End your day the same way, such as with a certain prayer or staring at the stars.

Retreating as a Group

Three or four people might want to take their retreat together by staying at the same location (with separate rooms for sleeping and just "being") and meeting a few times a day. This can be as varied as a few people at a retreat center or a bunch of guys on a fishing trip. All should agree on times to be alone and times to meet.

Sessions together might include one or two of these:

- Discussion of what happened during their times alone, how they heard God; this might include reading of what was written in their journals

- Mealtime
- Evenings of being together but being quiet, perhaps each reading or doing artwork or tending a campfire
- Saying a pre-bedtime, evening prayer together

Participants should guard each other's quiet and work hard at not being intrusive, respecting God's ability to speak to each of us.

Preparation for Your Retreat

Start gathering what you'll need, especially hiking gear and things for your creative outlets. Pray about how God might want to nurture you on this retreat. Ask someone who cares about you to pray for you while you're gone, especially if you're often plagued with worry or regret. Count on God's help to let go of those things.

Choosing a Retreat Site

Two important questions to consider are these:

- Do you want to fix your own food and eat by yourself (a secluded place or a retreat center hermitage), or would you rather be at a retreat center where you will eat with others three times a day?
- What sort of physical activity do you want to participate in (hiking, Jacuzzi-sitting, fishing)?

A retreat center is better than a resort getaway because it will promote quiet. It might have:

- A worshipping community of monks or nuns who invite you to join in certain short offices (services) throughout the day

- A fireplace that you might enjoy tending
- A piano you can play if you wish
- A spiritual director (if so, make those arrangements ahead and let the director know the topic you have chosen and how often you'd like to meet)

Can't I Retreat at Home?

Going away takes you away from distractions and gives you a different, more relaxed attitude. If you absolutely cannot get away (even for a morning in the park), remove all distractions (turn off telephones; do not turn on a computer or television; do not answer the door). Take everything that you will need to a place in your house or apartment that does not remind you of work and distractions. Keeping a lit candle in that room might help you quiet yourself and focus.

If you don't have much time when you'll be home alone, you might wish to do just one session a week. If so, try to go through the session the same day of the week and at the same time. This will develop a retreat rhythm in your life.

Reentry into Home, Family, and Community

Before leaving your retreat site, pause. Thank God for this extended time. As you near home, start picturing the people who might be there, what they need from you, and what your tasks will be. Thank God for these people and ask God to help you welcome them. Once you arrive, keep moving as slowly as possible.

As the days pass, continue to journal about the ideas you absorbed during the retreat. Reread your journal.

Make notes on what worked well about your personal retreat (location, setting, timing) so that your next retreat will bring an even more natural tendency to rest in God.

A God Who Speaks

Because God is always present with us — sleeping or eating, working or relaxing, worshipping or doing mundane chores — conversation with God is a normal part of life. Jesus invited us: "Come to me, learn from me, abide in me." In light of this, "we should be surprised if God did *not* speak to us."[1] We were built to share our life with God, not just to call on God to help us achieve our goal for today (a better parking place, a new job, changing someone we love).

God really does want to be with us and talk with us. We weren't meant to live our life by our own wits; the Holy Spirit guides us as a "personal mentor who longs to train us in the art of life in the Kingdom"[2] of God today, here and now. And so we come to the Word to dialogue with God. We live our life asking, seeking, and knocking on God's door. Then hearing God occurs naturally with those believers who live their life with God daily.

Opening to God's Message

Find a comfortable, pleasant spot to settle that will not present distractions to you.

First, why are you taking this retreat?

- A part of your life needs attention
- There is something you need to hear from God
- There is some change you need to make
- There is something God has been inviting you to recently
- Other _____

Set these reasons aside and don't let them consume your attention. By the time you're finished with the retreat, you might find they have been addressed without your trying to do so.

Second, to what degree do you think the following statements are true?

False   True
1 2 3 4 5

It hasn't occurred to people that God wants to communicate with them day in and day out, so they don't listen.

Some people dismiss the idea of hearing God because they're so turned off by people who claim to hear God constantly.

People think that getting answers from God is tricky business.

God is a VIP and talks to us only when we insist on it.

People view God as a vending machine: They ask God to deliver what they need (prayer requests) and they're unhappy when the answers don't come sliding down the vending machine slot.

If we don't communicate with God in average, everyday circumstances on a regular basis, it will be more difficult to communicate when we're in trouble or trying to make a decision.

God actively pursues a relationship with us, setting up creation to speak to us even if we don't think to listen otherwise.

*Dialogue with God is not only possible, it is essential. Ability to hear our
Teacher is a necessary part of being one of Jesus' disciples.
There is great joy in discovering experientially that God
really wants to be with us and talk with us.*
—DAVID TAKLE

Immersed in God's Message

Before reading the Scripture passage, consider these ideas.

BACKGROUND ABOUT DAVID: David had an interactive
life with God. Perhaps it began when as a young man herding sheep
he had to tend them carefully and fight off dangerous animals. In this
solitary work, he responded to God in words that became psalms or
seeds of later psalms attributed to him. He did this long before the
Spirit of the Lord came upon him in power (see 1 Samuel 16:13).

No one expected David to be anointed by Samuel to be king;
it seemed to have surprised his family and probably him as well. As
the anointed future king, he continued tending sheep and acting as a
musician. In the upcoming 1 Chronicles passage, David has become
king and has just led the Israelites in victory over the Philistines, who
were their oppressors. Before this, the Philistines had defeated the
Israelites under King Saul.

DAVID'S PRAYERS: Although few instances of David praying
are recorded in Scripture, David's interactive life with God is displayed
in more than seventy-five psalms attributed to David. In one of these
psalms, God is quoted as saying, "I will instruct you and teach you
in the way you should go; I will counsel you and watch over you"
(Psalm 32:8). So when David heard from God as described in the
1 Chronicles passage, it wasn't a spectacular or unusual occurrence;
it was a communication from God, David's life mentor, with whom
he was used to conversing. David's hearing God occurred within a

whole life of dialogue with God (of praise and celebration, of thankfulness, of pleading, even of weeping with God).

Before reading the Scripture passage, move through this exercise to quiet and focus yourself. (Once you learn it, you can shut your eyes and say it.)

> Be still and know that God is God. *Pause.*
> Be still and know that God. *Pause.*
> Be still and know. *Pause.*
> Be still. *Pause.*
> Be.

Read the passage aloud slowly.

When the Philistines heard that David had been anointed king over all Israel, they went up in full force to search for him, but David heard about it and went out to meet them. Now the Philistines had come and raided the Valley of Rephaim; so David inquired of God: "Shall I go and attack the Philistines? Will you hand them over to me?"

The LORD answered him, "Go, I will hand them over to you."

So David and his men went up to Baal Perazim, and there he defeated them. He said, "As waters break out, God has broken out against my enemies by my hand." So that place was called Baal Perazim. The Philistines had abandoned their gods there, and David gave orders to burn them in the fire.

Once more the Philistines raided the valley; so David inquired of God again, and God answered him, "Do not go straight up, but circle around them and attack them in front of the balsam trees. As soon as you hear the sound of marching in the tops of the balsam trees, move out to battle, because that will mean God has gone out in front of you to strike the Philistine army." So David did as God commanded him, and they struck down the Philistine army, all the way from Gibeon to Gezer. (1 Chronicles 14:8-16)

Before reading the passage again, consider the following ideas.

ENTERING INTO THE SCENE: Feel the hurt and anger of the Israelites from the Philistines' repeated raids, which consisted of stealing, burning, and killing. As the new king, David probably mourned the harm the Philistines did to his people. He may have even hated them. He easily could have let these feelings interfere with what he *thought* he heard as God's directions. Imagine David smelling the smoke from the fires that burned the Philistines' gods, ridding the earth of what is false but shortly afterward hearing that the Philistines have again raided the valley.

Consider how the soldiers felt about God's personal "come alongside" method of giving them victory. The soldiers *heard* the sounds of God. Ponder that a minute. When have you heard sounds that you knew for sure were sounds originated solely by God? It was as if God marched *with* them but also *out in front of* them as the actual commander of their army. This was a "with God" moment they probably thought about on their beds when they went to sleep each night and never forgot for the rest of their lives.

Imagine the soldiers waiting to move out, knowing that the sound that would signal them to attack would be God's marching in the tops of trees next to them. (This is one of the oddest yet sweetest of God's interventions.) These Israelite soldiers—possibly very young and very old but all likely tired of defending their land from the Philistines and watching friends and relatives die — agree to follow behind and under an unseen sound of marching that comes from a not-human origin.

Pause for a moment:

- What do you think the marching they heard sounded like? (Try to imitate the sound.)
- How would you (as a soldier) have felt when you heard it?
- How would you (as a soldier) have felt days later when you tried to explain this to your village, your spouse, your children or grandchildren?

As you read the passage again, consider what word or phrase stands out most to you or a moment in the account that stands out to you (perhaps as David or a soldier or even a Philistine soldier). Cautions:

- Waiting for a word to stand out is not a spooky or magical thing. This is a natural thing that probably already happens to you when you read the Bible. You think, *How come I never saw that word or phrase or idea before?* Actually, you did see it before, but now you see it in a new and different way. It now stands out to you.
- Don't feel pressured to make something up. If nothing stands out, quiet yourself, read the quieting exercise ("In our meditation we ponder the chosen text . . .") and read the Scripture passage again.
- Don't use self-directed effort to try to apply the passage to yourself. When you attempt to apply a passage, you try to figure out what you should do to implement what you read. At this point, simply let God bring to you what you need to know. Let it be God's effort, not your own.
- Be open to letting God speak to you. Expect to be surprised.

Reread the passage again slowly (either aloud or silently). Don't choose what stands out to you; let it come to you as you become open to being in the passage.

When the Philistines heard that David had been anointed king over all Israel, they went up in full force to search for him, but David heard about it and went out to meet them. Now the Philistines had come and raided the Valley of Rephaim; so David inquired of God: "Shall I go and attack the Philistines? Will you hand them over to me?"

The LORD answered him, "Go, I will hand them over to you."

So David and his men went up to Baal Perazim, and there he defeated them. He said, "As waters break out, God has broken out against my enemies by my hand." So that place was called Baal Perazim. The Philistines had abandoned their gods there, and David gave orders to burn them in the fire.

Once more the Philistines raided the valley; so David inquired of God again, and God answered him, "Do not go straight up, but circle around them and attack them in front of the balsam trees. As soon as you hear the sound of marching in the tops of the balsam trees, move out to battle, because that will mean God has gone out in front of you to strike the Philistine army." So David did as God commanded him, and they struck down the Philistine army, all the way from Gibeon to Gezer.

Write down the word or phrase or idea that stands out most to you.

What thoughts or impressions come to you? What connections do you make? What questions or perhaps objections do you have? Does anything surprise you?

What might God be saying to you through what has stood out in this passage?

Responding to God's Message

Read the passage again to yourself and consider how it leads you to dialogue with God.

> When the Philistines heard that David had been anointed king over all Israel, they went up in full force to search for him, but David heard about it and went out to meet them. Now the Philistines had come and raided the Valley of Rephaim; so David inquired of God: "Shall I go and attack the Philistines? Will you hand them over to me?"
> The LORD answered him, "Go, I will hand them over to you."

So David and his men went up to Baal Perazim, and there he defeated them. He said, "As waters break out, God has broken out against my enemies by my hand." So that place was called Baal Perazim. The Philistines had abandoned their gods there, and David gave orders to burn them in the fire.

Once more the Philistines raided the valley; so David inquired of God again, and God answered him, "Do not go straight up, but circle around them and attack them in front of the balsam trees. As soon as you hear the sound of marching in the tops of the balsam trees, move out to battle, because that will mean God has gone out in front of you to strike the Philistine army." So David did as God commanded him, and they struck down the Philistine army, all the way from Gibeon to Gezer.

Write your prayer response in the space provided or say it aloud. Doing so will make it more concrete and relational. Be open to having a dialogue with God, to being gently led by the Holy Spirit. You might want to begin with "Dear God" or "Dear Jesus." Never feel pressed to write pages and pages. One sentence might really be enough, or you may need to write more. If you're not sure how to start, here are some possibilities:

- Begin with, "I'm so glad that you said . . ." or "I really needed to hear that you . . ."
- Write what you would have wanted to pray if you had been an Israelite soldier (or David) in this passage.
- Ask God questions and mark them because you may find them answered by the end of today or tomorrow.
- Feel free to say things that don't sound spiritual (such as, "I envy David for getting such a specific answer from you" or "I envy David for knowing you so well"). Then move on with more you need to say.

- Use words or ideas from this psalm that describe the sort of life David lived that made it possible for him to hear God so well:

> O LORD, you have searched me
> > and you know me.
> You know when I sit and when I rise;
> > you perceive my thoughts from afar.
> You discern my going out and my lying down;
> > you are familiar with all my ways.
> Before a word is on my tongue
> > you know it completely, O LORD.
> You hem me in—behind and before;
> > you have laid your hand upon me.
> Such knowledge is too wonderful for me,
> > too lofty for me to attain. (Psalm 139:1-6)

Resting in God in the Message

If you wish, read the passage again to yourself one more time and rest in what you experienced.

As you've read the passage several times, how have you experienced God? What was God like? Reflect on how God seemed to you. Did you have a sense that you're only talking to yourself or that God was present? Did God seem distant or attentive? Caring or frustrated? Demanding or inviting? Talk to God about this.

Allow yourself time to soak in what has come to you—questions, new ideas, and clarifications about God or yourself. Let it sink all the way down to where you really live. Sit for a few moments and ponder what has transpired. You might wish to:

- Sit and just "be" with God.
- Appreciate or celebrate what you believe that God said in your conversation and who God was in it.
- Worship God in some way (even dancing, singing a favorite song, or drawing).
- Rest in the idea that God wants to communicate with you and is always reaching out to engage you.

Close this interaction with God with a prayer you particularly like or this prayer (from John Baillie's *A Diary of Private Prayer*):

> Give me an *open ear*, O God, that I may hear Thy voice calling me to high endeavour. Too often have I been deaf to the appeals Thou hast addressed to me, but now give me courage to answer, *Here am I, send me.*

Give me an *open mind*, O God, a mind ready to receive and
to welcome such new light of knowledge as it is Thy will
to reveal to me.[3]

Move into a time of enjoying the life and breath God gave you.
You might want to:

- Take a nap
- Take a walk, hike, swim, or do relaxing exercises
- Try "porch sitting," watching birds and trees, or sitting in a Jacuzzi
- Do a creative activity (using art materials, woodworking, needlework, beadwork), without trying to accomplish anything
- Do light, meditative reading (not a detective novel or something that engages you wholly)

Cultivating Quietness

Hearing and conversing with God is something we have to *learn* how to do. We aren't born knowing how any more than we're born recognizing the voice of our parents or caregivers. Over time, we learn to recognize God's voice through experience and experimentation (even by recognizing what is *not* God's voice). Jesus believed in practice sessions, evidenced by how he spoke to the disciples through the Holy Spirit after he had risen from the dead but before he ascended: "In my former book, Theophilus, I wrote about all that Jesus began to do and to teach until the day he was taken up to heaven, *after giving instructions through the Holy Spirit* to the apostles he had chosen" (Acts 1:1-2, emphasis added). Even though Jesus was with his disciples physically at that time, he had them practice hearing his instructions *through the Holy Spirit.*

On the other hand, we don't have to do anything unusual or strange to hear God, but it is important to cultivate an inner quietness. That doesn't just happen; we must learn how to still ourselves, trust God, and live the life of Jesus on this earth. Once we have an inner quietness, instances of hearing God will most often occur in quiet, attentive prayer and unhurried Bible reading. We can't make God speak to us, and we should never try to do that, but we can simply remain open to the voice of the One we love.

> *It is much more important to cultivate the quiet, inward space*
> *of a constant listening than to always be approaching God*
> *for specific direction.*
> —DALLAS WILLARD

Opening to God's Message

Settle in the same space as the last conversation unless that proved to be distracting. (If the previous session is still resonating with you, pause for a moment. Do you want to do it again? If so, this is what retreatants call "repetitions." You might need to go deeper or broader.)

Begin to focus on cultivating quietness by pondering the following:

What distractions in life make it most difficult for me to have an inner quietness?

When praying or reading the Bible, what is most likely to keep me from being attentive?

What is most helpful to me in eliminating either of these distractions?

During prayer or Bible reading, our inner distractions are usually wandering thoughts. That's why it helps to identify the "committee members" that live in our head, chattering away at us. For example, they might be: the *rescuer*, who distracts us from quietness to trying to solve other people's problems; the *picture perfect* person in us, who tries to be perfect and wants others to be; the *victim* in us, who chafes at others' inflictions; the *defender* in us, who wants to explain or tell people off; the *critic* in us, who scrutinizes others.[1] They are not the voice of God but of your unregenerated self (see Psalm 13:2). Even when you quiet them, they will keep coming back. Don't scold yourself; just send them away again.

Try to name your inner committee members. They might imitate people you have loved or revered, such as the well-meaning but whiny, grouchy relative or the demeaning, demanding teacher.

Immersed in God's Message

BACKGROUND: In Psalm 37, the psalmist cries out to God. In the second passage, Jesus describes himself as the Good Shepherd and speaks about how his "sheep" relate to him.

WAITING: Waiting on God is frequently thought to be impatiently standing by until God (belatedly) provides what we need. People speak of being in the "waiting room with God" as a heavy, burdensome thing. In contrast, Scripture links the ideas of *waiting* and *hoping* so that waiting is happily done with hopeful expectation: "My soul, wait silently for God alone, for my expectation is from Him" (Psalm 62:5, NKJV). So "waiting on God" is being attentive to God, such as being still and knowing that God is God (see Psalm 46:10). It is closely associated with delighting in God, which means resting in God's presence and gazing at the goodness of God.

Before reading the Scripture passage, move through this exercise to quiet and focus yourself. (Once you learn it, shut your eyes and say it.)

> Be still and know that God is God. *Pause.*
> Be still and know that God. *Pause.*
> Be still and know. *Pause.*
> Be still. *Pause.*
> Be.

Read the passage aloud slowly.

> Do not fret because of evil men
>   or be envious of those who do wrong;
> for like the grass they will soon wither,
>   like green plants they will soon die away.
>
> Trust in the LORD and do good;
>   dwell in the land and enjoy safe pasture.
> Delight yourself in the LORD
>   and he will give you the desires of your heart.

Commit your way to the LORD;
    trust in him and he will do this:
He will make your righteousness shine like the dawn,
    the justice of your cause like the noonday sun.

Be still before the LORD and wait patiently for him;
    do not fret when men succeed in their ways,
    when they carry out their wicked schemes. . . .

The meek will inherit the land
    and enjoy great peace. . . .

The man who enters by the gate is the shepherd of his sheep. The watchman opens the gate for him, and the sheep listen to his voice. He calls his own sheep by name and leads them out. When he has brought out all his own, he goes on ahead of them, and his sheep follow him because they know his voice. . . .

    My sheep listen to my voice; I know them, and they follow me. (Psalm 37:1-7,11; John 10:2-4,27)

Before reading the passage again, consider:
PATTERN OF THE PSALMIST PRAYER: This psalmist models the process of stilling oneself. Notice this pattern:

- Choosing not to worry about what other people are doing; setting aside thoughts about them (see verses 1-2,7)
- Naming the emotion that is ruling you (envy) and setting its cause aside for God to take care of (see verses 1-2)
- Choosing to trust God (see verses 3,5)
- Focusing on pictures of safety (see verse 3)

- Delighting in God (see verse 4)
- Looking forward to what God will provide (see verses 7,11)
- Being still before God (see verse 7)
- Waiting on God instead of letting prayer degenerate into "holy worry" (see verse 7)

This pattern of stilling oneself includes the dismissing of negative thoughts (the committee members) as well as delighting in God and waiting on God in a quiet, prayerful way. Before you read the passages again, consider if you need to do any of the listed things to quiet or still yourself. Or perhaps you'd like to use music or repeat a favorite verse that helps you be mindful of God's presence in order to cultivate quietness.

A SHEPHERD'S WAY OF LEADING: Jesus described himself as a shepherd who is personal and calls the sheep by name (see John 10:2-4,27). This shepherd is not pushy; he doesn't get behind the sheep and shove him but moves ahead and calls back to him to follow. The shepherd expects the sheep to be learning his voice and understanding how important it is to follow that voice.

ENTERING INTO THE PASSAGE: As you read the Scripture this next time, notice what feelings come over you. How do your feelings change as the psalm passage (and you) become quieter and quieter? How do you feel about following the shepherd, listening to his voice, being with the shepherd?

READING SCRIPTURE ALOUD: Consider reading the psalm phrases differently according to the content. For example, you may wish to read verses 1 and 2 loudly but verses 3, 4, 7, and 8 more quietly. Consider whispering the word *Selah* and pausing after you say it.

As you read the passage aloud, listen for the word or phrase that resonates with you or the scene or image that stays with you. Remember:

- Don't feel pressured to make something up. If nothing stands out, quiet yourself and try it again.
- Don't use self-directed effort to try to apply the passage to yourself. When you attempt to apply a passage, you try to figure out what you should do to implement what you read. At this point, simply let God bring to you what you need to know. Let it be God's effort, not your own.
- Be open to letting God speak to you. Expect to be surprised.

Do not fret because of evil men
    or be envious of those who do wrong;
for like the grass they will soon wither,
    like green plants they will soon die away.

Trust in the LORD and do good;
    dwell in the land and enjoy safe pasture.
Delight yourself in the LORD
    and he will give you the desires of your heart.

Commit your way to the LORD;
    trust in him and he will do this:
He will make your righteousness shine like the dawn,
    the justice of your cause like the noonday sun.

Be still before the LORD and wait patiently for him;
    do not fret when men succeed in their ways,
    when they carry out their wicked schemes. . . .

The meek will inherit the land
    and enjoy great peace. . . .

The man who enters by the gate is the shepherd of his sheep. The watchman opens the gate for him, and the sheep listen to his voice. He calls his own sheep by name and leads them out. When he has brought out all his own, he goes on ahead of them, and his sheep follow him because they know his voice. . . .

My sheep listen to my voice; I know them, and they follow me.

Write down the word, phrase, or idea that stands out to you.

What thoughts or impressions come to you about that word or phrase? What connections do you make? What questions or perhaps objections do you have? How does the word or phrase surprise you?

What might God be saying to you through what has stood out in this passage?

Responding to God's Message

Read the passage again to yourself and consider how it leads you to dialogue with God. Write down whatever you wish to pray. Be open to having a dialogue with God, to being gently led by the Holy Spirit. You may wish to tell God how you feel about following the shepherd and learning that voice. Or you may want to pray certain phrases of the psalm but then embellish them with ideas that are specific to you.[2] Never feel pressed to write pages and pages. One sentence might really be enough, or you may need to write more.

Try saying portions of the passage aloud, as if God were saying the words to you. Start with the following paraphrase, but adjust it as it seems appropriate.

As you pray, _____ (your name), you don't need to worry about anything, especially what others have or what they're doing wrong. They look daunting but their efforts will fade.

Trust me, _____ (your name), and do good; dwell with me and enjoy safety. Delight yourself in me because I AM the true desire of your heart. Commit all your ways—big and small—to me. Trust me and I will bring forth in you a deep goodness that shines with bright purity like intense sunlight.

Quiet yourself with me; wait patiently with expectancy to sense my presence.

Don't get upset when people who seem selfish are successful—those who surrender to me will have everything they
need and enjoy great peace.

(Jesus speaking to you) I am your shepherd—your guide
and protector in all of life. It's safe for me to come to be with
you, and I want you to learn to listen for me to speak to you.
I'll speak to you individually, sometimes even by name, and
I'll lead you to know what to do. I'll be a little in front of you
so you are never lost. You'll get so you like following me and
knowing my voice. All those who are mine listen to my voice;
I know them, and they follow me.

Resting in God in the Message

Read the passage again to yourself one more time or simply go over the
words or phrases that stood out to you.

As you've read the passage several times, how have you experienced God? What was God like? Reflect on how God seemed to you.
Did you have a sense that you're only talking to yourself or that God
was present? Did God seem distant or attentive? Caring or frustrated?
Demanding or inviting? Talk to God about this.

Allow yourself time to soak in what has come to you—questions,
new ideas, and clarifications about God or yourself. Let it sink all the
way down to where you really live. Sit for a few moments and ponder
what has transpired. You might wish to:

- Sit and just "be" with God.
- Appreciate or celebrate what you believe that God said in your
  conversation and who God was in it.

- Worship God in some way (even dancing, singing a favorite song, or drawing).
- Take a walk and ponder what it would be like to follow behind someone like Jesus, having him call you by name and watch out for you, guiding you along.
- Rest in the idea that God wants to communicate with us and this is part of how our life with God is formed.
- When it's dark, take a Bible and flashlight outside and read Psalm 37 to God. You might also wish to:
  - Commit verse 7 to your short-term memory and whisper a personalized version of it to God when you're finished ("I will be still before you and wait patiently for you!").
  - Set down the flashlight, raise your arms high in the air to God, and belt out verse 4 (from memory): "I will delight myself in you, and I shall have the desire of my heart, which is you most of all").

Close this interaction with God with a prayer you particularly like or this prayer (from John Baillie's *A Diary of Private Prayer*):

Give me an *open ear*, O God, that I may hear Thy voice calling me to high endeavour. Too often have I been deaf to the appeals Thou hast addressed to me, but now give me courage to answer, *Here am I, send me.*

Give me an *open mind*, O God, a mind ready to receive and to welcome such new light of knowledge as it is Thy will to reveal to me.[3]

Move into a time of enjoying the life and breath God gave you. You might want to:

- Take a nap
- Take a walk, hike, swim, or do relaxing exercises

- Try "porch sitting," watching birds and trees, or sitting in a Jacuzzi
- Do a creative activity (using art materials, woodworking, needlework, beadwork), without trying to accomplish anything
- Do light, meditative reading (not a detective novel or something that engages you wholly)

The Content of God's Speech

Now and then you've heard someone say, "God told me . . ." You might have wondered, *Was that really God they heard, or just themselves having God say what they want to hear?* If we think we're hearing something from God, we can test it by making sure it's consistent with the content of Scripture. Specifically, it's wise to compare it with what God ordinarily and customarily does and says, not the things that might be considered exceptions or individual circumstances.

That's why it's helpful to be familiar with the kinds of things God says to people in Scripture. Pay special attention to repeated phrases and major themes of Scripture. Even when looking at biblical examples, focus on the ideas behind them rather than the details because God as your mentor and teacher will supply different and important details for you. For example, praying without your head covered can usually be done in good conscience, but praying with a proud, irreverent spirit cannot (which is what the uncovered head signified in that culture; see 1 Corinthians 11:2-16). God led the Israelites to fight to subdue Canaan only at a certain time (after some years had passed) and in a certain way. That never happened again.

Expect the content to be individualized according to both your needs and your blind spots. Those who love to spend money might hear God urge them to cut back and be content with less. Those who are stingy and too frugal might hear God invite them to celebrate more. The Holy Spirit knows what we need, while we are often oblivious to our shortcomings.

We will also hear God better if we speak transparently in our dialogue with God. We need to come clean with God about our self-serving motives and ask God to help us be open to better ones. Otherwise, people claim to hear the wildest things from God and condone them as scriptural: running off with a neighbor's wife (supposedly *love*), cheating on income tax (supposedly *thriftiness*), or using guilt to manipulate people into helping us (supposedly *service*). This is a case of trying to hear what we think will benefit us. In reality, this is not love, thriftiness, or service but lust, greed, and exploitation. That's why we need to separate the voices in our mind (the committee) from the just and merciful God of the universe. When muddled, we need to ask a wise friend, *Is this me or is this God?* When in doubt, wait.

We must not be misled by wishful thinking. We are going to go through
the mill of life like everyone else. We who are disciples
are different because we also have a higher or additional life —
a different quality of life, a spiritual life, an eternal life —
not because we are spared the ordinary troubles that
befall ordinary human beings.
—DALLAS WILLARD

Opening to God's Message

Settle in the same space as before unless that proved to be distracting. (If the previous session is still resonating with you, pause for a moment. Do you want to do it again?)

From what you know about Scripture, what would you say are the four or five big things God thinks about and cares about?

Which of these do you think God is most likely to speak to you about (because of your neediness in that area)?

In what kinds of ways does God communicate with you?

- Telling you what you did wrong or expressing disappointment in what you did wrong
- Helping you see someone else's heart (how that person feels inside and how he or she approaches life)
- Nudging you to go the extra mile with someone
- Laughing at you for your silliness
- Giving you ideas about how to love someone next to you
- Helping you find lost items or remembering what you need to say
- Urging you to watch the sunset
- Other _____
- Other _____

What does how you answered tell you about how God seems to you? About how you may have distorted God's approach to you?

Immersed in God's Message

BACKGROUND: The Old Testament Prophets, which makes up nearly one-fourth of the Bible, does very little of foretelling the future. Instead, much of it records God speaking to nations and individuals in one of these two ways: (1) clarifying what has gone wrong; and (2) offering hope for making it right.[1] Prophets generally critiqued problems and sought to energize people to move forward with God. The passages from our Scripture reading represent three major themes of God's speech throughout Scripture:

- Offering intimacy and comfort (see Isaiah 43:1-2,5)
- Nudging people forward to act (see Isaiah 52:1-2,10-11)
- Confronting people in their errors (see Isaiah 58:4,6-8)

Before reading the Scripture passage, move through this exercise to quiet and focus yourself. (Once you learn it, shut your eyes.)

Be still and know that God is God. *Pause.*

Be still and know that God. *Pause.*

Be still and know. *Pause.*

Be still. *Pause.*

Be.

Read this passage aloud slowly (but not the headings or references).

OFFERING INTIMACY AND COMFORT

Fear not, for I have redeemed you;
    I have summoned you by name; you are mine.

When you pass through the waters,
>   I will be with you;
and when you pass through the rivers,
>   they will not sweep over you.
When you walk through the fire,
>   you will not be burned;
>   the flames will not set you ablaze. . . .
Do not be afraid, for I am with you;
>   I will bring your children from the east
>   and gather you from the west. . . .

NUDGING FORWARD IN MINISTRY

Awake, awake, O Zion,
>   clothe yourself with strength. . . .
Shake off your dust;
>   rise up, sit enthroned, O Jerusalem.
Free yourself from the chains on your neck,
>   O captive Daughter of Zion. . . .

The LORD will lay bare his holy arm
>   in the sight of all the nations,
and all the ends of the earth will see
>   the salvation of our God.

Depart, depart, go out from there!
>   Touch no unclean thing!
Come out from it and be pure,
>   you who carry the vessels of the LORD. . . .

CHALLENGING AND CONFRONTING

Your fasting ends in quarreling and strife,
    and in striking each other with wicked fists.
You cannot fast as you do today
    and expect your voice to be heard on high. . . .

Is not this the kind of fasting I have chosen:
to loose the chains of injustice
    and untie the cords of the yoke,
to set the oppressed free
    and break every yoke?
Is it not to share your food with the hungry
    and to provide the poor wanderer with shelter—
when you see the naked, to clothe him,
    and not to turn away from your own flesh and blood?
Then your light will break forth like the dawn,
    and your healing will quickly appear;
then your righteousness will go before you,
    and the glory of the LORD will be your rear guard.
        (Isaiah 43:1-2,5; 52:1,2,10-11; 58:4,6-8)

Before reading the passage again, consider:

BACKGROUND: It is generally agreed that chapters 40–66 of Isaiah are to have been addressed to the Jews living in exile in Persia after the Babylonian captivity. Many of them longed to go home to Israel, but others didn't think about returning. Some adhered to Jewish beliefs and traditions, while others strayed.

OFFERING INTIMACY AND COMFORT: Because the exiles had endured persecution, they needed comfort and reminders of intimacy with God. Throughout Scripture, God offers comfort and intimacy to many people, including the rejected Hagar and a reluctant Moses (see Genesis 21:17; Exodus 3:12). Jesus often comforted his disciples and Paul the churches (see John 14; 2 Thessalonians 2:16-17).

NUDGING FORWARD IN MINISTRY: Through Isaiah, God seeks to energize the forlorn Jews to be ready to return from exile just as God often urges people to move from their place of inactivity (Abram from Ur, see Genesis 12; the Israelites from wandering in the wilderness, see Deuteronomy 1:6-8). God loves to bring light into dark situations and asks us to be a part of that (see Genesis 1:3,22; 2 Corinthians 4:6).

CHALLENGING AND CONFRONTING: The Jews' wrong-hearted fast ended in quarreling and arrogance and didn't cause them to show mercy and justice to the impoverished people around them. God (sometimes through prophets) shows the way forward, combining clarity with hope as God challenged King David in his sin and Jonah in his prejudice (see 1 Chronicles 28:3; Jonah 4:9,11) as well as Adam and Eve, Cain, and Saul (see Genesis 3:13; 4:10; 1 Samuel 13:11). Jesus challenged both the Pharisees and his disciples (see Matthew 23; Luke 22:24-30). Such challenge and confrontation need not be shameful; instead, God helps these much-loved people to see themselves truly and then points them in the right direction.

God's challenges are often reiterations of primary commands in Scripture, such as the Ten Commandments and the Great Commandment: to love God with all one's self and to love one's neighbor as one's self. God isn't always heavy-handed in this; instead, a gentle whisper comes to us saying, "What would it look like to love X in the next ten minutes?" X might be the competitive coworker, the officer giving you a speeding ticket, the customer service rep who doesn't help you, or the annoying child who lives next door.

OTHER THINGS GOD SAYS: Less frequently in Scripture God also:

- Tests people (Abraham to sacrifice Isaac, see Genesis 22:2)
- Grieves over the wickedness of nations and people (in Noah's

time, see Genesis 6:6; Babylon and Egypt's wickedness, see
Isaiah 23:12; 47:1; Jeremiah 46:11)

- Refrains from speaking or addressing an issue because delay is
in our best interest ("How long?" occurs twenty-two times in
Psalms)

GO OR STAY?: Most people are eager to hear God only when
they have a decision to make. They come to God to get a signal: go
or stay; left or right; north or south; A or B. Yet very little Scripture
describes God telling specific people to do specific things. God does
not restrict conversations with us to only big decisions or help in trouble. God wants to be in continual conversation with us, guiding us in
all of life.

If we have a conversational life with God, we'll normally find we
don't get to these enormous crossroads. Instead, God guides along the
way. Before we come to a crossroads, we have a pretty good idea of
what to do. But without this conversational life with God, people don't
know how to listen to God, so every crossroads becomes a crisis.

ENTERING INTO THE PASSAGE: Consider how it would feel
to be part of a "remnant" population, surviving within a culture from
which you differ drastically. The Jewish exiles in Persia were a remnant
of the Israelite population that honored God and acted to make God
known, but they were living within the Persian culture that glamor-
ized outward appearance and achievements.

As you read the passages, be careful not to choose which section or
what words speak to you most. Try to be open to letting God speak to
you in needy places within you that you are oblivious to. Perhaps you
have been an exile in ways you haven't considered and need words of
hope and clarity. Read slowly and carefully; then shut your eyes, notic-
ing which word or phrase comes to you and stays with you.

Fear not, for I have redeemed you;
    I have summoned you by name; you are mine.

When you pass through the waters,
　　I will be with you;
and when you pass through the rivers,
　　they will not sweep over you.
When you walk through the fire,
　　you will not be burned;
　　the flames will not set you ablaze. . . .
Do not be afraid, for I am with you;
　　I will bring your children from the east
　　and gather you from the west. . . .

Awake, awake, O Zion,
　　clothe yourself with strength. . . .
Shake off your dust;
　　rise up, sit enthroned, O Jerusalem.
Free yourself from the chains on your neck,
　　O captive Daughter of Zion. . . .

The LORD will lay bare his holy arm
　　in the sight of all the nations,
and all the ends of the earth will see
　　the salvation of our God.

Depart, depart, go out from there!
　　Touch no unclean thing!
Come out from it and be pure,
　　you who carry the vessels of the LORD. . . .

Your fasting ends in quarreling and strife,
　　and in striking each other with wicked fists.
You cannot fast as you do today
　　and expect your voice to be heard on high. . . .

Is not this the kind of fasting I have chosen:
to loose the chains of injustice
    and untie the cords of the yoke,
to set the oppressed free
    and break every yoke?
Is it not to share your food with the hungry
    and to provide the poor wanderer with shelter—
when you see the naked, to clothe him,
    and not to turn away from your own flesh and blood?
Then your light will break forth like the dawn,
    and your healing will quickly appear;
then your righteousness will go before you,
    and the glory of the LORD will be your rear guard.

Write down the word, phrase, or idea that stands out to you.

What thoughts or impressions come to you about that word or phrase or idea? What connections do you make? What questions or perhaps objections do you have? Does anything surprise you?

What might God be saying to you through what has stood out in this passage?

Responding to God's Message

Read the passage again to yourself or read only the phrase that stood out to you and the surrounding verses. Consider how doing so leads you to dialogue with God.

> Fear not, for I have redeemed you;
>> I have summoned you by name; you are mine.
> When you pass through the waters,
>> I will be with you;
> and when you pass through the rivers,
>> they will not sweep over you.
> When you walk through the fire,
>> you will not be burned;
>> the flames will not set you ablaze. . . .
> Do not be afraid, for I am with you;
>> I will bring your children from the east
>> and gather you from the west. . . .
>
> Awake, awake, O Zion,
>> clothe yourself with strength. . . .
> Shake off your dust;
>> rise up, sit enthroned, O Jerusalem.
> Free yourself from the chains on your neck,
>> O captive Daughter of Zion. . . .
>
> The LORD will lay bare his holy arm
>> in the sight of all the nations,
> and all the ends of the earth will see
>> the salvation of our God.
>
> Depart, depart, go out from there!
>> Touch no unclean thing!

Come out from it and be pure,
  you who carry the vessels of the LORD. . . .

Your fasting ends in quarreling and strife,
  and in striking each other with wicked fists.
You cannot fast as you do today
  and expect your voice to be heard on high. . . .

Is not this the kind of fasting I have chosen:
to loose the chains of injustice
  and untie the cords of the yoke,
to set the oppressed free
  and break every yoke?
Is it not to share your food with the hungry
  and to provide the poor wanderer with shelter—
when you see the naked, to clothe him,
  and not to turn away from your own flesh and blood?
Then your light will break forth like the dawn,
  and your healing will quickly appear;
then your righteousness will go before you,
  and the glory of the LORD will be your rear guard.

Ponder those words, phrases, or ideas that stood out to you and say back to God what you most need to say today. Be open to having a dialogue with God, to being gently led by the Holy Spirit. If you're not sure how to start, here are some possibilities:

- Begin with, "I am a remnant person because . . ."
- Answer any questions you think God might be asking you or ask God questions.
- Thank God for comforting you and offering you intimacy.

- Respond to how God is nudging you forward into action. You might ask God to show you your next step.
- Regarding any challenges or confrontations, ask God to show you your next step.

Resting in God in the Message

As you've read the passage several times, how have you experienced God? What was God like? Reflect on how God seemed to you. Did you have a sense that you're only talking to yourself or that God was present? Did God seem distant or attentive? Caring or frustrated? Demanding or inviting? Talk to God about this.

Allow yourself time to soak in what has come to you — questions, new ideas, and clarifications about God or yourself. You might wish to:

- Sit and just "be" in the comfort of God's companionship, even if you're also being confronted or nudged forward in ministry.
- Appreciate or celebrate what you believe that God said in your conversation and who God was in it.
- Worship God in some way (even dancing, singing a favorite song, or drawing).
- Rest in the idea that God wants to communicate with us and this is part of how our life with God is formed.

Close this interaction with God with a prayer you particularly like or this prayer (from John Baillie's *A Diary of Private Prayer*):

Give me an *open ear*, O God, that I may hear Thy voice calling me to high endeavour. Too often have I been deaf to the appeals Thou hast addressed to me, but now give me courage to answer, *Here am I, send me.*

Give me an *open mind*, O God, a mind ready to receive and to welcome such new light of knowledge as it is Thy will to reveal to me.[2]

Give me an *open mind*, O God, a mind ready to receive and to welcome such new light of knowledge as it is Thy will to reveal to me.[2]

Move into a time of enjoying the life and breath God gave you. You might want to:

- Take a nap
- Take a walk, hike, swim, or do relaxing exercises
- Try "porch sitting," watching birds and trees, or sitting in a Jacuzzi
- Do a creative activity (using art materials, woodworking, needlework, beadwork), without trying to accomplish anything
- Do light, meditative reading (not a detective novel or something that engages you wholly)

The Tone of God's Voice

Many times people say, "God told me . . ." and then engage in the same self-scolding you've heard them reproach themselves with before. One way to discern whether we're hearing God's voice is by listening to the tone of it. We ask ourselves, Does the spirit and quality of that voice sound like my normal self-talk, or is it a little surprising and just right?

Is [the tone of God's voice] slow or fast, smooth or halting in its flow, indirect or to the point? A voice may be passionate or cold, whining or demanding, timid or confident, coaxing or commanding. This is . . . a matter of personal characteristics that become tangibly present in the voice. [God's voice] is a spirit of exalted peacefulness and confidence, of joy, of sweet reasonableness, and of will for the good.
—DALLAS WILLARD

In this conversation, we examine how to hear God better by looking at the tone of God's voice—the quality and spirit of God's way of speaking. Even when the tone of God's voice is bold or firm, it still flows from God's character of love: patient, kind, not bragging or prideful, not rude or self-seeking, not easily irritated; keeping no record of wrongs; not delighting in evil but rejoicing with truth (see 1 Corinthians 13:4-7). God knows how to "[speak] the truth in love" (Ephesians 4:15); God can be angry yet show great love, which means that if God wants to say something firm to you, God can do it with great kindness.

This leads us to examine the tone of voice we superimpose on God's speech as we read God's words in Scripture. That tone needs to match God's character.

Opening to God's Message

Settle in the same space as before unless that proved to be distracting. (If the previous session is still resonating with you, pause for a moment. Do you want to do it again? If so, this is what retreatants call "repetitions." You might need to go deeper or broader.)

Read the following list twice. The first time you read it, become familiar with the words. The second time you read it, circle the five words that best communicate how the tone of God's voice sounds most often to you. Please be honest. Also, cross out the five words that describe what you least hear reflected in the tone of God's voice.

loud	comforting	demanding	restful	indescribable
friendly	unintelligible	quiet	frightful	intimate
sensible	astounding	caring	forceful	impatient
willing to listen	insistent	peaceful	critical	encouraging
confident	complaining	hurried	relaxed	moralizing
inquisitive	strict	easily irritated	gentle	dogmatic

Why did you choose the words you chose?

Immersed in God's Message

BACKGROUND: James, as Jesus' brother or cousin, grew up hearing Jesus' voice most days of his life: in the carpenter shop, in the out-of-doors walking to work sites, at home during meals, in friendly horseplay, and in the synagogue. Also, James describes "wisdom from above," which Jesus personified. No doubt he learned this from Jesus' example.

Psalm 103 describes not only what God is like but also what God is not like. This is helpful because it exposes our misinterpretations of God.

Before reading, move through this exercise to quiet and focus yourself.

Be still and know that God is God. *Pause.*
Be still and know that God. *Pause.*
Be still and know. *Pause.*
Be still. *Pause.*
Be.

Read this Scripture passage aloud very slowly, paying special attention to the first verse.

The wisdom from above is first pure, then peaceable, gentle, willing to yield, full of mercy and good fruits, without a trace of partiality or hypocrisy. . . .

Bless the LORD, O my soul,
>   and do not forget all his benefits—
who forgives all your iniquity,
>   who heals all your diseases,
who redeems your life from the Pit,
>   who crowns you with steadfast love and mercy,
who satisfies you with good as long as you live
>   so that your youth is renewed like the eagle's. . . .

The LORD is merciful and gracious,
>   slow to anger and abounding in steadfast love.
He will not always accuse,
>   nor will he keep his anger forever.
He does not deal with us according to our sins,
>   nor repay us according to our iniquities.
For as the heavens are high above the earth,
>   so great is his steadfast love toward those who fear him;
as far as the east is from the west,
>   so far he removes our transgressions from us.
As a father has compassion for his children,
>   so the LORD has compassion for those who fear him.
>   (James 3:17; Psalm 103:2-5,8-13, NRSV)

Before reading the passage again, consider:
MEANING OF WORDS: Consider how the following words
from James 3:17 are translated in other Bible versions:

- Considerate: gentle and reasonable (MSG)
- Willing to yield: easy to be entreated (KJV)
- Without a trace of partiality or hypocrisy: not hot one day and
  cold the next, not two-faced (MSG)

DISCERNMENT ISSUES TO CONSIDER: One reason the tone of God's speaking is so important is that we often hear God through the recurring thoughts in our mind. As stated in the introduction regarding being with God in the Word, we don't always know where God's words leave off and our thoughts begin.

It's easy to tell that some thoughts are not from God, such as: Flirt with your neighbor's spouse; eat too much; try to impress your boss. But other thoughts sound good—are they all from God? For example, we often mistake all "shoulds," such as calling someone to see how they're doing, as being from God. The tone is our clue. If it's a nagging, demanding tone, it's probably not from God but our thoughts in the form of a "committee member" (see conversation 2) such as the "picture perfect" person who nags you and uses guilt to get you to do things. Now, calling this person may be a very good thing to do, but we're concerned with learning to discern the voice of God. So our first step with a recurrent thought is to listen to the tone of the recurrent thought: Is it nagging (probably not God) or respectful? Does it reflect "wisdom from above" or something else?

One of the clues that it's not a committee member is that it surprises you. It doesn't sound in content or tone like anything the unregenerate parts of you (the committee) would ever come up with. Instead, it sounds refreshingly sensible and gentle.

If the thought is merely a committee member speaking up, it needs to be dismissed because it will continually distract us from God. After ushering that committee member to the door, we can quiet ourselves and fellowship with God. We might even dialogue with God: *What do I need to know about the person I think I should call?* See what comes to you. God may or may not be nudging you to call them on the telephone; perhaps God is nudging you to pray for them or visit them instead. The point of this retreat is to discern God's leading. That will require not being deceived into thinking that every good and kind thing that is to be done on the planet is yours to do.

Read the passage aloud again. Consider what word, phrase, or idea resonates with you, stays with you, or seems to shimmer for you. What do you need to know about the tone, spirit, and quality in which God routinely speaks?

> The wisdom from above is first pure, then peaceable, gentle, willing to yield, full of mercy and good fruits, without a trace of partiality or hypocrisy. . . .

> Bless the LORD, O my soul,
>   and do not forget all his benefits—
> who forgives all your iniquity,
>   who heals all your diseases,
> who redeems your life from the Pit,
>   who crowns you with steadfast love and mercy,
> who satisfies you with good as long as you live
>   so that your youth is renewed like the eagle's. . . .

> The LORD is merciful and gracious,
>   slow to anger and abounding in steadfast love.
> He will not always accuse,
>   nor will he keep his anger forever.
> He does not deal with us according to our sins,
>   nor repay us according to our iniquities.
> For as the heavens are high above the earth,
>   so great is his steadfast love toward those who fear him;
> as far as the east is from the west,
>   so far he removes our transgressions from us.
> As a father has compassion for his children,
>   so the LORD has compassion for those who fear him.

Write down the word, phrase, or idea that stands out to you.

What thoughts or impressions come to you about that word or phrase? What connections do you make? What questions or perhaps objections do you have? How does the word or phrase surprise you?

What might God be saying to you through what has stood out in this passage?

When you have been reading Scripture, have you been hearing God's voice within the tones described in this passage, or have you been ascribing to God's voice a tone that is not described here?

Responding to God's Message

Read the passage again to yourself and consider how it leads you to dialogue with God.

The wisdom from above is first pure, then peaceable, gentle, willing to yield, full of mercy and good fruits, without a trace of partiality or hypocrisy. . . .

Bless the LORD, O my soul,
  and do not forget all his benefits—
who forgives all your iniquity,
  who heals all your diseases,
who redeems your life from the Pit,
  who crowns you with steadfast love and mercy,
who satisfies you with good as long as you live
  so that your youth is renewed like the eagle's. . . .

The LORD is merciful and gracious,
  slow to anger and abounding in steadfast love.
He will not always accuse,
  nor will he keep his anger forever.
He does not deal with us according to our sins,
  nor repay us according to our iniquities.
For as the heavens are high above the earth,
  so great is his steadfast love toward those who fear him;
as far as the east is from the west,
  so far he removes our transgressions from us.
As a father has compassion for his children,
  so the LORD has compassion for those who fear him.

Write your prayer response in the space provided or say it aloud. Doing so will make it more concrete and relational. Be open to having a dialogue with God, to being gently led by the Holy Spirit. What do you need to say to God about how you hear God (or anything else)? Some possibilities:

- Tell God how you haven't been hearing well and would like to hear better.
- Begin with, "I'm so glad that you said . . ." or "I really needed to hear that you . . ."

- Tell God the part of wisdom from above you most admire. What would that look like in you?

Resting in God in the Message

Read the Scripture passage again to yourself one more time.

As you've read the passage several times, how have you experienced God? What was God like? Reflect on how God seemed to you, especially if God seemed pure, peaceable, gentle, willing to yield, full of mercy and good fruits, without a trace of partiality or hypocrisy. Talk to God about this.

Allow yourself time to soak in what has come to you — questions, new ideas, and clarifications about God or yourself. Let it sink all the way down to where you really live. Sit for a few moments and ponder what has transpired. You might wish to:

- Sit and just "be" with God.
- Praise God for being pure love and goodness and for speaking with pure love.
- Lie on the floor with arms raised and bless God.
- Appreciate or celebrate what you believe that God said in your conversation and who God was in it.
- Worship God in some way (even dancing, singing a favorite song, or drawing).
- Rest in the idea that God wants to communicate with us and this is part of how our life with God is formed.

Close this interaction with God with a prayer you particularly like or this prayer (from John Baillie's *A Diary of Private Prayer*):

Give me an *open ear*, O God, that I may hear Thy voice calling me to high endeavour. Too often have I been deaf to the appeals Thou hast addressed to me, but now give me courage to answer, *Here am I, send me.*

Give me an *open mind*, O God, a mind ready to receive and to welcome such new light of knowledge as it is Thy will to reveal to me.[1]

Move into a time of enjoying the life and breath God gave you. You might want to:

- Take a nap
- Take a walk, hike, swim, or do relaxing exercises
- Try "porch sitting," watching birds and trees, or sitting in a Jacuzzi
- Do a creative activity (using art materials, woodworking, needlework, beadwork), without trying to accomplish anything
- Do light, meditative reading (not a detective novel or something that engages you wholly)

The Still, Small Voice

lthough some people seek to be guided by astrology or tarot cards, God communicates mostly through words and speaking. This relational approach has always been primary. The Bible is full of instances of God speaking directly to people such as Moses and Paul and lesser-known figures such as Ezekiel and Ananias (who helped Saul/Paul, see Acts 9). Some people write off the act of God speaking to individuals as only an Old Testament occurrence (which is a shame because the Old Testament demonstrates so well how God interacts with individuals), yet the New Testament is full of similar instances, especially the church's history book Acts.

Most often, people hear God speak to them when they are involved in shared activity with God. Paul heard God's direction while on his missionary journey; Philip heard God in the midst of preaching in Samaritan villages. If we're continually focused on self—getting ahead, making an impression, improving ourselves—we probably won't hear God because God will not, generally speaking, "compete for our attention. Occasionally a Saul gets knocked off his horse. But we must expect that God will not run over us."[1] But when we live a life with God (see conversation 1), we live in a rhythm of asking, seeking, and knocking, so we will normally hear some sort of reply—not always through an audible voice, but through the Holy Spirit or a still, small inner voice that comes into our mind.

Opening to God's Message

Settle in the same space as before unless that proved to be distracting. (If the previous session is still resonating with you, pause for a moment. Do you want to do it again? If so, this is what retreatants call "repetitions." You may need to go deeper or broader.)

When have you felt like saying, "I have had enough, Lord"?

Immersed in God's Message

BACKGROUND: Our passage begins by saying that Elijah was afraid. Ahab and Jezebel, monarchs of Israel, worshipped Baal, a foreign god that Elijah prophesied against. Elijah challenged the prophets of Baal to a contest in which Elijah proved God's power by calling down fire from heaven to consume his sacrifice. Baal's prophets got no response to their sacrifice and "lost" the contest. After Elijah's stunning victory, Jezebel angrily threatened his life. Elijah believed he was the only prophet left because Jezebel had ordered the death of all the Lord's prophets (see 1 Kings 18:4).

SETTING: Elijah runs the length of Israel from north to south (ninety miles). From there, he continues traveling for forty days to Mount Horeb in the southern tip of Arabia (two hundred to three hundred miles, depending on the route).[2] Mount Horeb refers to the mountainous Mount Sinai area where God conversed with Moses at the burning bush and later gave the Israelites the Ten Commandments.

Before reading, move through this exercise to quiet yourself and remove any distracting thoughts.

Be still and know that God is God. *Pause.*
Be still and know that God. *Pause.*
Be still and know. *Pause.*
Be still. *Pause.*
Be.

Read this Scripture passage aloud slowly.

[Elijah] arose and ran for his life, and went to Beersheba, which *belongs* to Judah, and left his servant there. But he himself went a day's journey into the wilderness, and came and sat down under a broom tree. And he prayed that he might die, and said, "It is enough! Now, LORD, take my life, for I *am* no better than my fathers!"

Then as he lay and slept under a broom tree, suddenly an angel touched him, and said to him, "Arise *and* eat." Then he looked, and there by his head *was* a cake baked on coals, and a jar of water. So he ate and drank, and lay down again. And the angel of the LORD came back the second time, and touched him, and said, "Arise *and* eat, because the journey *is* too great for you." So he arose, and ate and drank; and he went in the strength of that food forty days and forty nights as far as Horeb, the mountain of God.

And there he went into a cave, and spent the night in that place; and behold, the word of the LORD *came* to him, and He said to him, "What are you doing here, Elijah?"

So he said, "I have been very zealous for the LORD God

of hosts; for the children of Israel have forsaken Your covenant, torn down Your altars, and killed Your prophets with
the sword. I alone am left; and they seek to take my life."

Then He said, "Go out, and stand on the mountain before
the LORD. And behold, the LORD passed by, and a great and
strong wind tore into the mountains and broke the rocks in
pieces before the LORD, *but* the LORD *was* not in the wind;
and after the wind an earthquake, *but* the LORD *was* not in
the earthquake; and after the earthquake a fire, *but* the LORD
was not in the fire; and after the fire a still small voice.

So it was, when Elijah heard *it,* that he wrapped his face
in his mantle and went out and stood in the entrance of the
cave. Suddenly a voice *came* to him, and said, "What are you
doing here, Elijah?"

And he said, "I have been very zealous for the LORD God
of hosts; because the children of Israel have forsaken Your covenant, torn down Your altars, and killed Your prophets with
the sword. I alone am left; and they seek to take my life."

Then the LORD said to him: "Go, return on your way to
the Wilderness of Damascus; and when you arrive, anoint
Hazael *as* king over Syria." (1 Kings 19:3-15, NKJV)

Before reading the passage again, consider these ideas:
PICTURING THE PASSAGE: Try to picture Elijah sitting under
the broom tree, which is a large shrub that can grow up to thirteen
feet high. Also, picture him with his garment made of hair-cloth and
a wide belt.

Picture also an angel who cooks a "power bar" type of food — bread
baked over hot coals — that sustains Elijah for forty days. Can you
smell the fire cooking the bread? Notice how practical the angel's ministry is: food, water, sleep, and very little conversation. That's part of
what a retreat is about.

If you spent the night in a cave, what might you see or hear? What do caves smell like? How would you feel being in the cave?

Stand with Elijah as he watches the earthquake and the powerful wind tearing the mountains apart and shattering the rocks. Feel yourself squatting down or hiding because you are unable to stand up in the wind and as the earth moves under you. Feel the heat and hear the loud crackling noises of the fire as rocks explode in front of you.

Then finally hear the "still small voice" (NKJV) or "gentle whisper" (NIV) or "sound of sheer silence" (NRSV).

ELIJAH'S EMOTIONS: After Elijah's successful mountaintop experience, he received a death threat. What would living with a death threat feel like? Elijah became suicidal. Again, try to remember when you have felt like saying, "I've had enough, Lord."[3]

God is always speaking. To hear his voice is not usually a mystical experience. It consists merely of a willingness to pay heed to the God who lays a claim on our lives. For the word hear *in the New Testament does not commonly refer to an auditory experience. More often it means "to pay heed."*
—JOHN WHITE

GOD'S CONVERSATION CONTENT (the kinds of things God says to people):

- Questions: "What are you doing here, Elijah?" Why do you think God likes to ask us questions?
- Directions for further conversation: "Go out, and stand on the mountain . . ."
- Tasks to do to bring people into shared activity: "Anoint Hazael . . . Jehu . . . and Elisha."

As you read the passage aloud again slowly, allow yourself to enter the scene, perhaps as Elijah or an onlooker. Just be open to being in the passage and letting God speak to you. What moment, word, or phrase stands out to you?

[Elijah] arose and ran for his life, and went to Beersheba, which *belongs* to Judah, and left his servant there. But he himself went a day's journey into the wilderness, and came and sat down under a broom tree. And he prayed that he might die, and said, "It is enough! Now, LORD, take my life, for I *am* no better than my fathers!"

Then as he lay and slept under a broom tree, suddenly an angel touched him, and said to him, "Arise *and* eat." Then he looked, and there by his head *was* a cake baked on coals, and a jar of water. So he ate and drank, and lay down again. And the angel of the LORD came back the second time, and touched him, and said, "Arise *and* eat, because the journey *is* too great for you." So he arose, and ate and drank; and he went in the strength of that food forty days and forty nights as far as Horeb, the mountain of God.

And there he went into a cave, and spent the night in that place; and behold, the word of the LORD *came* to him, and He said to him, "What are you doing here, Elijah?"

So he said, "I have been very zealous for the LORD God of hosts; for the children of Israel have forsaken Your covenant, torn down Your altars, and killed Your prophets with the sword. I alone am left; and they seek to take my life."

Then He said, "Go out, and stand on the mountain before the LORD. And behold, the LORD passed by, and a great and strong wind tore into the mountains and broke the rocks in pieces before the LORD, *but* the LORD *was* not in the wind; and after the wind an earthquake, *but* the LORD *was* not in the earthquake; and after the earthquake a fire, *but* the LORD *was* not in the fire; and after the fire a still small voice.

So it was, when Elijah heard *it,* that he wrapped his face in his mantle and went out and stood in the entrance of the cave. Suddenly a voice *came* to him, and said, "What are you doing here, Elijah?"

And he said, "I have been very zealous for the LORD God of hosts; because the children of Israel have forsaken Your covenant, torn down Your altars, and killed Your prophets with the sword. I alone am left; and they seek to take my life."

Then the LORD said to him: "Go, return on your way to the Wilderness of Damascus; and when you arrive, anoint Hazael *as* king over Syria."

What moment in the story (or word or phrase) stood out to you? Write it down.

What feelings did you have as Elijah or the onlooker? Write these down.

What might God be saying to you through what has stood out in this passage?

Responding to God's Message

Read the Scripture passage again, to yourself this time, and consider how it leads you to dialogue with God.

[Elijah] arose and ran for his life, and went to Beersheba, which *belongs* to Judah, and left his servant there. But he himself went a day's journey into the wilderness, and came and sat down under a broom tree. And he prayed that he might die, and said, "It is enough! Now, Lord, take my life, for I *am* no better than my fathers!"

Then as he lay and slept under a broom tree, suddenly an angel touched him, and said to him, "Arise *and* eat." Then he looked, and there by his head *was* a cake baked on coals, and a jar of water. So he ate and drank, and lay down again. And the angel of the Lord came back the second time, and touched him, and said, "Arise *and* eat, because the journey *is* too great for you." So he arose, and ate and drank; and he went in the strength of that food forty days and forty nights as far as Horeb, the mountain of God.

And there he went into a cave, and spent the night in that place; and behold, the word of the Lord *came* to him, and He said to him, "What are you doing here, Elijah?"

So he said, "I have been very zealous for the Lord God of hosts; for the children of Israel have forsaken Your covenant, torn down Your altars, and killed Your prophets with the sword. I alone am left; and they seek to take my life."

Then He said, "Go out, and stand on the mountain before the Lord. And behold, the Lord passed by, and a great and strong wind tore into the mountains and broke the rocks in pieces before the Lord, *but* the Lord *was* not in the wind; and after the wind an earthquake, *but* the Lord *was* not in the earthquake; and after the earthquake a fire, *but* the LORD *was* not in the fire; and after the fire a still small voice.

So it was, when Elijah heard *it,* that he wrapped his face in his mantle and went out and stood in the entrance of the cave. Suddenly a voice *came* to him, and said, "What are you doing here, Elijah?"

And he said, "I have been very zealous for the LORD God of hosts; because the children of Israel have forsaken Your covenant, torn down Your altars, and killed Your prophets with the sword. I alone am left; and they seek to take my life."

Then the LORD said to him: "Go, return on your way to the Wilderness of Damascus; and when you arrive, anoint Hazael *as* king over Syria."

Write your prayer response in the space provided or say it aloud. Be open to having a dialogue with God, to being gently led by the Holy Spirit. If you're not sure where to start, here are some possibilities:

- Begin with, "Like Elijah, I . . ."
- Begin in Elijah's persona: Tell God how you (as Elijah) respond to this adventure.
- Respond to God concerning why the still, small voice was a preferable way of speaking instead of through an earthquake, wind, or fire.
- Answer any questions you think God might be asking you.
- Ponder how God might be inviting you into shared activity (as God invited Elijah to share in anointing leaders).
- Feel free to say things that don't sound spiritual (such as, "I have had enough, Lord").

Resting in God in the Message

Read the passage again to yourself one more time.

As you've read the passage several times, how have you experienced God? What was God like? Reflect on how God seemed to you. Did God seem distant or attentive? Talk to God about this.

Allow yourself time to soak in what has come to you—questions, new ideas, and clarifications about God or yourself. Let it sink all the way down to where you really live. Sit for a few moments and ponder what has transpired. You might wish to:

- Sit and just "be" with God.
- Appreciate or celebrate what you believe that God said in your conversation and who God was in it.
- Rest in the idea that God wants to communicate with us and this is part of how our life with God is formed.
- Worship God in some way (even dancing, singing a favorite song, or drawing).
- Walk to where you can stand high above the woods, a valley, or even a city or perhaps to something that reminds you of a cave. Stand on an edge of earth or out in front of the "cave" and imagine what it would be like to have wind almost knock you down or to have fire come close to you or to almost lose your footing because of an earthquake. Stand fast with God.

Close this interaction with God with a prayer you particularly like or this prayer (from John Baillie's *A Diary of Private Prayer*):

> Give me an *open ear*, O God, that I may hear Thy voice calling me to high endeavour. Too often have I been deaf to the appeals Thou hast addressed to me, but now give me courage to answer, *Here am I, send me.*
>
> Give me an *open mind*, O God, a mind ready to receive and to welcome such new light of knowledge as it is Thy will to reveal to me.[4]

Move into a time of enjoying the life and breath God gave you. You might want to:

- Take a nap
- Take a walk, hike, swim, or do relaxing exercises
- Try "porch sitting," watching birds and trees, or sitting in a Jacuzzi
- Do a creative activity (using art materials, woodworking, needlework, beadwork), without trying to accomplish anything
- Do light, meditative reading (not a detective novel or something that engages you wholly)

God's Unusual Speech

God usually speaks to us within the quiet inner voice as we are paying attention to God in various ways: dialoguing with God in prayer, conversing with God in the Word, or adoring God through nature. Those are the most frequent ways.

Yet there are times when God chooses to communicate directly through dreams, visions, and miraculous manifestations (burning bushes and so on). These are the unusual (but intriguing and much-remembered) stories of Scripture: Only once did a donkey speak; only once did a fleece become miraculously dry or wet; only once did a wrestling angel visit a fearful man. These unusual methods point out how God interacts with people in ways most helpful to them. God might or might not speak to you in unusual ways. If so, it will fit you exactly and help you grow.

Opening to God's Message

Settle in your usual place. (If the previous session is still resonating with you, pause for a moment. Do you want to do it again? If so, this is what retreatants call "repetitions." You may need to go deeper or broader.)

When we think of God speaking to people in the Bible, we often think of the more spectacular moments such as these:

A VOICE PLUS A PHENOMENON

- A vision and a smoking firepot (to Abraham, see Genesis 15:1-21)
- A voice from a bush that didn't burn itself out (to Moses, see Exodus 3:1-22)
- A voice and the appearance of a dove (at Jesus' baptism, see Matthew 3:16-17)

ANGELS (WE OFTEN CAN'T TELL IF IT'S AN ANGEL OR THE LORD)

- Three angels came to Abraham's tent (although one was identified as "the LORD"; see Genesis 18:1-33).
- The commander of the Lord's army spoke to Joshua (see Joshua 5:13-15).
- An angel appeared to Hagar as she fled from Sarai (see Genesis 16:6-16).
- An angel appeared to Balaam as he gave in to greed (after his donkey spoke to him; see Numbers 22:22-35).
- An angel spoke to Gideon as he threshed grain in a winepress (see Judges 6:11-24).
- Angels appeared to many others including Samson's parents, Isaiah, Daniel, Zechariah, Mary, the women at the empty tomb, Peter being released from jail, and Paul as his ship was about to run aground (see Judges 13; Isaiah 6:6-13; Daniel 9:20-27; Luke 1:11-20; 1:26-38; Matthew 28:2-7; Acts 5:19-20; 27:23-26).

DREAMS AND VISIONS

- Joseph the patriarch dreamed predictive dreams as a young man (see Genesis 37:5-10).
- Joseph, the father of Jesus, had three dreams that told him how to secure Jesus' safety and well-being (see Matthew 1:20-25).
- Abraham's smoking firepot experience also included a vision (see Genesis 15:1-21).
- Ananias dreamed about going to minister to Saul (see Acts 9:10-16).
- Cornelius's vision came with a message to send for Peter; Peter's vision was of the unclean animals he was told to eat (see Acts 10:3-20).

Children love the spectacular and show themselves as children by actively seeking it out, running heedlessly after it. It may sometimes be given by God—it may be necessary—because of our denseness or our hardheartedness. However, it is never to be taken as a mark of spiritual adulthood or superiority. If spectacular things do come to them, those who are advanced in the Way of Christ never lightly discuss them or invoke them to prove that they are right or "with it" in some way.
—DALLAS WILLARD

AUDIBLE VOICE

- God spoke to Abraham about sacrificing Isaac; then an angel spoke to him to save Isaac (see Genesis 22:11-12).
- The young boy Samuel heard God and thought it was the priest Eli (see 1 Samuel 3:4-14).
- God spoke to Saul of Tarsus on the road to Damascus (see Acts 9:3-7); a light accompanied the audible voice.

- God spoke audibly at Jesus' baptism and transfiguration (see Matthew 3:16-17; Mark 9:7).

THROUGH PEOPLE
- Through Aaron to Israel (see Exodus 4:10-16)
- Through Paul who was not eloquent (see 1 Corinthians 2:1-5)
- Through unlearned and ignorant men (see Acts 4:13)

Which moment would you most like to have witnessed? Why?

Immersed in God's Message

CONTEXT: Abraham is "visited" by God in a strange way. At this point in Abraham's life, God has assured him many times that he will have a son and has explicitly said that the son will not be Ishmael but will be born to Sarah. At this, Abraham falls on his face and laughs, worshipping God with delight and wonder and saying, "Will a son be born to a man a hundred years old? Will Sarah bear a child at the age of ninety?" (see Genesis 17:17).

Before reading, move through this exercise to quiet and focus yourself.

> Be still and know that God is God. *Pause.*
> Be still and know that God. *Pause.*
> Be still and know. *Pause.*
> Be still. *Pause.*
> Be.

Read this Scripture passage aloud slowly.

The LORD appeared to Abraham near the great trees of Mamre while he was sitting at the entrance to his tent in the heat of the day. Abraham looked up and saw three men standing nearby. When he saw them, he hurried from the entrance of his tent to meet them and bowed low to the ground.

He said, "If I have found favor in your eyes, my lord, do not pass your servant by. Let a little water be brought, and then you may all wash your feet and rest under this tree. Let me get you something to eat, so you can be refreshed and then go on your way—now that you have come to your servant."

"Very well," they answered, "do as you say."

So Abraham hurried into the tent to Sarah. "Quick," he said, "get three seahs of fine flour and knead it and bake some bread."

Then he ran to the herd and selected a choice, tender calf and gave it to a servant, who hurried to prepare it. He then brought some curds and milk and the calf that had been prepared, and set these before them. While they ate, he stood near them under a tree.

"Where is your wife Sarah?" they asked him.

"There, in the tent," he said.

Then the Lord said, "I will surely return to you about this time next year, and Sarah your wife will have a son."

Now Sarah was listening at the entrance to the tent, which was behind him. Abraham and Sarah were already old and well advanced in years, and Sarah was past the age of childbearing. So Sarah laughed to herself as she thought, "After I am worn out and my master is old, will I now have this pleasure?"

Then the Lord said to Abraham, "Why did Sarah laugh and say, 'Will I really have a child, now that I am old?' Is anything too hard for the Lord? I will return to you at the appointed time next year and Sarah will have a son."

Sarah was afraid, so she lied and said, "I did not laugh."
But he said, "Yes, you did laugh." (Genesis 18:1-15)

Before reading the passage again, consider:

BACKGROUND: **Three men.** Eventually one is identified as "the LORD." In Genesis 19:1 the other two are identified as angels. Abraham himself seems unsure; he offers the angels food and they eat it, appearing to be human.

God often shows up in mystery and disguise. In Jesus' post-resurrection appearances, Mary Magdalene mistook him for a gardener and the two disciples walking to Emmaus didn't recognize him. When Jacob wrestled with the "man" whom some believe was the angel of the Lord and others think was the Lord, Jacob asks, "Who are you?" and the being replies, "Why do you ask?" as if Jacob knows. The purpose seems to be to help people absorb the experience. To encounter God full force would be too much for any of us. So we should not be surprised to look up (as Abraham did) and see God disguised with dusty feet, an empty stomach, and stimulating conversation. Many times we won't be sure we recognize "God," and we shouldn't be ashamed but live in eager wonder, as Abraham did.

ENTERING INTO THE PASSAGE: **Abraham's excitement.** Although welcoming strangers is required by Canaanite custom and later by Hebrew law (because of the desolation in this area, strangers might have died if not cared for) and recommended in Christian practice, Abraham seems extremely enthusiastic: He hurried and ran and instructed Sarah to make the bread "quick" (verse 6). Can you picture a ninety-nine-year-old man acting this way? In addition, he eagerly "bowed low to the ground" (verse 2).

Abraham's attentiveness to strangers. He stands near them under a tree, as they eat, illustrating, "Do not forget to entertain strangers, for by so doing some people have entertained angels without knowing it" (Hebrews 13:2). For those who wish to hear God, attentiveness to strangers is important. Even though Abraham had met with God many times, he still wasn't sure if the stranger was the Lord. We're not sure either.

Sarah's laughter. Two interpretations exist: (1) Sarah is full of disbelief and so the Lord scolds her through Abraham and catches her in a lie; (2) Sarah laughed in joy and wonder (as Abraham did in Genesis 17:17) not only at the possibility that her dream would come true of her very old body having a child but also at the idea of having sexual pleasure at her age. The Lord is eager to recognize Sarah's joy (similar to Abraham's) and doesn't want her to allow fear to force her to deny her joy.

Either way, the product of Abraham's and Sarah's joy and laughter is Isaac, which means "laughter." One commentator suggests that the change in their names (Abram to Abraham and Sarai to Sarah) was the simple addition of ha-ha (the sound of laughter) because God "put laughter into their very names . . . as though God were laughing with the parents-to-be."[1] In the second interpretation, laughter becomes a way that we worship God and celebrate divine goodness.

MEANING OF WORDS: *Hard* is translated *wonderful* elsewhere: "Is anything too wonderful for the LORD?" (NRSV). God's speaking is not hampered by our inadequacies or even sin, but God's speaking to us doesn't necessarily mean we are worthy or adequate. In Genesis 18, the Lord appears to Abraham and speaks to Sarah even though they previously tried to force God's plan by uniting Abraham and Hagar to produce Ishmael.

PICTURING THE PASSAGE: Envision a compound of huge tents that a rich man such as Abraham would have had. These were large sturdy structures with doors that flapped in the wind. Feel the heat (it's the hottest part of the day) and watch Abraham perspire as he hurries. Hear the noises of feet being washed, materials brought for resting, bread being made, and a calf being slaughtered and prepared.

Reread the passage again slowly (either aloud or silently). Allow yourself to enter the scene, perhaps as Abraham or Sarah or a servant or one of the angels. What moment, word, or phrase stands out to you? Don't choose that now. Just be open to being in the passage. Let God speak to you. Expect to be surprised.

The LORD appeared to Abraham near the great trees of Mamre while he was sitting at the entrance to his tent in the heat of the day. Abraham looked up and saw three men standing nearby. When he saw them, he hurried from the entrance of his tent to meet them and bowed low to the ground.

He said, "If I have found favor in your eyes, my lord, do not pass your servant by. Let a little water be brought, and then you may all wash your feet and rest under this tree. Let me get you something to eat, so you can be refreshed and then go on your way—now that you have come to your servant."

"Very well," they answered, "do as you say."

So Abraham hurried into the tent to Sarah. "Quick," he said, "get three seahs of fine flour and knead it and bake some bread."

Then he ran to the herd and selected a choice, tender calf and gave it to a servant, who hurried to prepare it. He then brought some curds and milk and the calf that had been prepared, and set these before them. While they ate, he stood near them under a tree.

"Where is your wife Sarah?" they asked him.

"There, in the tent," he said.

Then the LORD said, "I will surely return to you about this time next year, and Sarah your wife will have a son."

Now Sarah was listening at the entrance to the tent, which was behind him. Abraham and Sarah were already old and well advanced in years, and Sarah was past the age of childbearing. So Sarah laughed to herself as she thought,

"After I am worn out and my master is old, will I now have this pleasure?"

Then the LORD said to Abraham, "Why did Sarah laugh and say, 'Will I really have a child, now that I am old?' Is anything too hard for the LORD? I will return to you at the appointed time next year and Sarah will have a son."

Sarah was afraid, so she lied and said, "I did not laugh."

But he said, "Yes, you did laugh."

What word, phrase, moment, or feeling stands out to you in this passage? Who were you in the passage? Imagine it again and write down as much about it as you can.

What thoughts or impressions come to you? What connections do you make? What questions or perhaps objections do you have? Does anything surprise you?

What might God be saying to you through the moment that stood out to you in this passage? How are you being engaged or engaging life or someone or a circumstance in the same way? What do you need to know? (Don't force this or try to apply it to yourself. Let it come to you.) Take a few minutes to think about this.

Responding to God's Message

Read the passage again to yourself and consider how it leads you to dialogue with God.

> The LORD appeared to Abraham near the great trees of Mamre while he was sitting at the entrance to his tent in the heat of the day. Abraham looked up and saw three men standing nearby. When he saw them, he hurried from the entrance of his tent to meet them and bowed low to the ground.
>
> He said, "If I have found favor in your eyes, my lord, do not pass your servant by. Let a little water be brought, and then you may all wash your feet and rest under this tree. Let me get you something to eat, so you can be refreshed and then go on your way — now that you have come to your servant."
>
> "Very well," they answered, "do as you say."
>
> So Abraham hurried into the tent to Sarah. "Quick," he said, "get three seahs of fine flour and knead it and bake some bread."
>
> Then he ran to the herd and selected a choice, tender calf and gave it to a servant, who hurried to prepare it. He then brought some curds and milk and the calf that had been prepared, and set these before them. While they ate, he stood near them under a tree.
>
> "Where is your wife Sarah?" they asked him.
>
> "There, in the tent," he said.
>
> Then the LORD said, "I will surely return to you about this time next year, and Sarah your wife will have a son."
>
> Now Sarah was listening at the entrance to the tent, which was behind him. Abraham and Sarah were already old and well advanced in years, and Sarah was past the age of childbearing. So Sarah laughed to herself as she thought,

"After I am worn out and my master is old, will I now have this pleasure?"

Then the LORD said to Abraham, "Why did Sarah laugh and say, 'Will I really have a child, now that I am old?' Is anything too hard for the LORD? I will return to you at the appointed time next year and Sarah will have a son."

Sarah was afraid, so she lied and said, "I did not laugh."

But he said, "Yes, you did laugh."

Pray as you need to pray. Be open to having a dialogue with God, to being gently led by the Holy Spirit. You might do one or more of these things:

- Thank God—even celebrate—for the ways God has shown up in your life.
- Ask God to help you be more attentive to strangers.
- Speak out the thoughts or feelings you had that were similar to Abraham or Sarah's thoughts or feelings.
- Ask God some questions and mark them because you may find them answered by the time you get home.

Resting in God in the Message

Read the passage again to yourself one more time.

As you've read the passage several times, how have you experienced God? What was God like? Reflect on how God seemed to you. Talk to God about this.

Allow yourself time to soak in Abraham and Sarah's experience and in the questions, new ideas, and clarifications about God or yourself that have come to you. Let it sink all the way down to where you really live. Sit for a few moments and ponder what has transpired.

Close this interaction with God with a prayer you particularly like or this prayer (from John Baillie's *A Diary of Private Prayer*):

Give me an *open ear*, O God, that I may hear Thy voice calling me to high endeavour. Too often have I been deaf to the appeals Thou hast addressed to me, but now give me courage to answer, *Here am I, send me.*

Give me an *open mind*, O God, a mind ready to receive and to welcome such new light of knowledge as it is Thy will to reveal to me.[2]

Move into a time of enjoying the life and breath God gave you. You might want to:

- Take a nap
- Take a walk, hike, swim, or do relaxing exercises
- Try "porch sitting," watching birds and trees, or sitting in a Jacuzzi
- Do a creative activity (using art materials, woodworking, needlework, beadwork), without trying to accomplish anything
- Do light, meditative reading (not a detective novel or something that engages you wholly)

Hearing God in the Word

W hen are we most likely to hear God? Although any time is a possibility (even in the middle of a workday, as God spoke to Moses in the burning bush as he herded sheep), we are most likely to engage in dialogue with God as we read the Word. This is even more likely to occur if we have an inner quietness in our reading (see conversation 2). This means that we are open to what God might say instead of assuming we already know what God has to say. It means that we are not preoccupied or rushed or hoping to get to the bottom of the page. As our relationship with God grows, we become more attentive to God speaking in the Word of God.

Opening to God's Message

Settle in your usual place. If you find you're distracted by this being your last session, soothe yourself by noting that this session is about being slow and attentive to God.

Pretend you are part of a group that had just heard God's Word read aloud. Let's say someone asked all of you what you heard from

God (not theology but God speaking to them) and everyone has sensed God speaking to them. Would that surprise you?

This is a small part of the issue addressed in the parable of the sower, in which Jesus presented four kinds of soil. Only one kind of soil produced a crop. This rich, loose, aerated soil is free of rocks and thorns, and that allows seeds to grow at great depth. The parable makes us wonder how we become such aerated soil instead of the hardened path, which doesn't receive the seed and so the birds eat it; the rocky soil, which produces rootless overnight plants in shallow soil that are scorched in the sun the next day; or the soil infested with thorns that choke the plant (see Matthew 13:3-9).

Some people are able to hear God speak to them in God's Word and others are not. Why do you think some do not hear? If you need some help to get thinking, pick from these ideas about why some don't hear, but then keep pondering.

- They're interested in other things such as getting on with their day or talking to people after church (hardened soil).
- They think that words of Scripture *sound good*, but their life is full of problems (rocky soil).
- They have too many things to think about, so they're unable to settle in and hear (thorn-choked soil).
- Other _____
- Other _____

What do you think is needed in order to hear God in God's Word?

Immersed in God's Message

Before reading, move through this exercise to quiet and focus yourself.

> Be still and know that God is God. *Pause.*
> Be still and know that God. *Pause.*
> Be still and know. *Pause.*
> Be still. *Pause.*
> Be.

Read this Scripture passage aloud slowly.

Welcome with meekness the implanted word that has the power to save your souls. . . .

Don't fool yourself into thinking that you are a listener when you are anything but, letting the Word go in one ear and out the other. *Act* on what you hear! Those who hear and don't act are like those who glance in the mirror, walk away, and two minutes later have no idea who they are, what they look like.

But whoever catches a glimpse of the revealed counsel of God—the free life!—even out of the corner of his eye, and sticks with it, is no distracted scatterbrain but a man or woman of action. That person will find delight and affirmation in the action. (James 1:21, NRSV; 22-25, MSG)

MEANING OF WORDS: *Welcome with meekness* is also translated "humbly accept" (NIV) or "in gentleness receive" (Barclay). These words describe the person with a "truly teachable spirit . . . not blinded by its own overmastering prejudices but . . . clear-eyed to the truth."[1]

> *[The Bible] is not only a book which was once spoken, but a book*
> *which is now speaking. . . . If you would follow on to know*
> *the Lord, come at once to the open Bible expecting*
> *it to speak to you. Do not come with the notion that*
> *it is a thing which you can push around*
> *at your convenience.*
> —A. W. TOZER

Our passage is urging a respectful, open-minded reading of Scripture rather than proof-texting or assuming we already know what it's saying. This is about reading the words anew *every single time*.

MEANING OF WORDS: *Implanted* is also translated *inborn* (Barclay) and *engrafted* (KJV). This word sometimes means "innate" (as opposed to acquired) and other times it means "planted in, as a seed in the ground." Both ideas work well: Interactive knowledge from the Word of God "comes from the depths of our being, the Spirit of God, the teaching of Christ and the preaching of men."[2]

MEANING OF WORDS: *Sticks with it* is also translated *continues* (NIV) or *persevere* (NRSV). This same word (*parameno*) means to "be permanent, persevere" and is often translated "abide."[3]

To *stick with* or *continue* or *persevere* or *abide* in the Word points to the need to soak in the words, phrases, and ideas of Scripture instead of getting through it so we can finish the chapter or go on to the next thing. To hear or read the words of Scripture is not enough; we need to listen with the ear of our heart to what God might be saying to us in the words of Scripture. As we learn to *abide* and *continue* in the words of God all day, surprising thoughts come to us when we're doing tasks that don't call for a lot of mental effort: gardening, running errands, cleaning the house, and mowing the lawn.

What color or gesture communicates the following?

- This gentle and humble welcoming of God's Word into ourselves

- This in-depth planting within the soul
- This soaking in, continuing in, abiding in the Word activity

Describe here your three colors or gestures. If you wish, do the gestures.

PICTURING THE PASSAGE: You might wish to envision yourself having a conversation with James, that one who knew Jesus so well and went on to lead the Jerusalem church and was later martyred. You've just heard James tell you to be "quick to hear" and "slow to speak" (James 1:19, NRSV), so you ask him, *What do you mean "quick to hear"?* This passage is his answer.

As you read the passage, consider what word, phrase, or idea resonates with you or stays with you.

Welcome with meekness the implanted word that has the power to save your souls. . . .

Don't fool yourself into thinking that you are a listener when you are anything but, letting the Word go in one ear and out the other. *Act* on what you hear! Those who hear and don't act are like those who glance in the mirror, walk away, and two minutes later have no idea who they are, what they look like.

But whoever catches a glimpse of the revealed counsel of God — the free life! — even out of the corner of his eye, and sticks with it, is no distracted scatterbrain but a man or woman of action. That person will find delight and affirmation in the action.

After reading the passage, write down the word or phrase that stood out to you or the feelings you may have had as a disciple.

What thoughts or impressions come to you about that word, phrase, or idea? What connections do you make? What questions or perhaps objections do you have? Does anything surprise you?

What might God be saying to you through what has stood out in this passage?

Responding to God's Message

Read the Scripture passage again to yourself. Then pray the passage and consider how it leads you to dialogue with God.

Here's an example of what praying the Scripture looks like.

SCRIPTURE TEXT	PRAYING the SCRIPTURE
Welcome with meekness the implanted word that has the power to save your souls.	O God, help me to full-heartedly, open-handedly welcome your words to be planted deep within me and deliver me from my self-centered tendencies.
Don't fool yourself into thinking that you are a listener when you are anything but, letting the Word go in one ear and out the other. *Act* on what you hear!	Help me not to merely listen to the Word — in one ear and out the other — so I've done my duty; help me to soak in it so that I *become* what it says and embody it within my actions.
Those who hear and don't act are like those who glance in the mirror, walk away, and two minutes later have no idea who they are, what they look like.	I confess that I have been like someone who looks at my face in a mirror, feels mildly horrified, but walks away and forgets about it.
But whoever catches a glimpse of the revealed counsel of God — the free life! — even out of the corner of his eye, and sticks with it, is no distracted scatterbrain but a man or woman of action.	I want to look intently into your words of life and catch glimpses of the counsel you reveal. I want to penetrate these words of life with my eyes and mind and heart so that I can't and don't want to forget them, so that they become part of me and my actions.
That person will find delight and affirmation in the action.	I know I will live a very different kind of life if I do this, so blessed and living in your companionship.

Now feel free to write (actually pray) your own version. Be open to having a dialogue with God, to being gently led by the Holy Spirit.

SCRIPTURE TEXT	PRAYING the SCRIPTURE
Welcome with meekness the implanted word that has the power to save your souls.	
Don't fool yourself into thinking that you are a listener when you are anything but, letting the Word go in one ear and out the other. *Act* on what you hear!	

Those who hear and don't act are like those who glance in the mirror, walk away, and two minutes later have no idea who they are, what they look like.	
But whoever catches a glimpse of the revealed counsel of God — the free life! — even out of the corner of his eye, and sticks with it, is no distracted scatterbrain but a man or woman of action.	
That person will find delight and affirmation in the action.	

Resting in God in the Message

Read the passage again to yourself one more time.

As you've read the passage several times, how have you experienced God? What was God like? Reflect on how God seemed to you. Talk to God about this.

Allow yourself time to soak in what has come to you — questions, new ideas, and clarifications about God or yourself. Let it sink all the way down to where you really live. Sit for a few moments and ponder what has transpired. You might wish to:

- Sit and just "be" with God, soaking in what God has said to you.
- Appreciate or celebrate what you believe God said in your conversation and who God was in it.
- Worship God in some way (even dancing, singing a favorite song, or drawing).
- Rest in the idea that God wants to communicate with us and this is part of how our life with God is formed.

Close this interaction with God with a prayer you particularly like or this prayer (from John Baillie's *A Diary of Private Prayer*):

Give me an *open ear*, O God, that I may hear Thy voice calling me to high endeavour. Too often have I been deaf to the appeals Thou hast addressed to me, but now give me courage to answer, *Here am I, send me.*

Give me an *open mind*, O God, a mind ready to receive and to welcome such new light of knowledge as it is Thy will to reveal to me.[4]

As you consider your transition back into normal life, think about:

- What you most need to know
- What you most need to celebrate
- What you most need to remember about hearing God in your life

Before leaving your retreat site, pause. Thank God for this extended time. As you near home, start picturing the people who might be there, what they need from you, and what your tasks will be. Thank God for these people and ask God to help you welcome them. Once you arrive, keep moving as slowly as possible.

As you make your way home, ponder also what worked well about your personal retreat (location, setting, timing) so that your next retreat will bring an even more natural tendency to rest in God. Don't forget to continue to reflect on the retreat. Some of your best insights may be yet to come.

Notes

Introduction: Why Retreat? Making Space for God

1. David Takle, *The Truth About Lies and the Lies About Truth* (Pasadena, CA: Shepherd's House, 2008), 174.
2. Takle, 174.
3. Lynne Baab, "A Day Off from God Stuff," *Leadership Journal*, Spring 2007, http://www.christianitytoday.com/le/2007/002/18.34.html.

Conversation 1: A God Who Speaks

1. Dallas Willard, *Hearing God: Developing a Conversational Relationship with God* (Downers Grove, IL: InterVarsity, 1999), 65.
2. David Takle, *The Truth About Lies and the Lies About Truth* (Pasadena, CA: Shepherd's House, 2008), 160.
3. John Baillie, *A Diary of Private Prayer* (New York: Scribner, 1949), 63, italics added.

Conversation 2: Cultivating Quietness

1. This is explained in much more detail in my book *When the Soul Listens: Finding Rest and Direction in Contemplative Prayer* (Colorado Springs, CO: NavPress, 1999), 127–128.
2. This method is called "festooning" and is described by C. S. Lewis in *Letters to Malcolm* (New York: Harcourt, 1992), 25.
3. John Baillie, *A Diary of Private Prayer* (New York: Scribner, 1949), 63.

Conversation 3: The Content of God's Speech

1. This theme is fleshed out in Walter Brueggemann, *The Prophetic Imagination* (Philadelphia: Fortress, 1978), 44–108.
2. John Baillie, *A Diary of Private Prayer* (New York: Scribner, 1949), 63.

Conversation 4: The Tone of God's Voice

1. John Baillie, *A Diary of Private Prayer* (New York: Scribner, 1949), 63.

Conversation 5: The Still, Small Voice

1. Dallas Willard, *Hearing God: Developing a Conversational Relationship with God* (Downers Grove, IL: InterVarsity, 1999), 90–91.
2. D. Guthrie and J. A. Motyer, *The New Bible Commentary* (Grand Rapids, MI: Eerdmans, 1991).
3. John White, *Daring to Draw Near* (Downers Grove, IL: InterVarsity, 1977), 14.
4. John Baillie, *A Diary of Private Prayer* (New York: Scribner, 1949), 63.

Conversatio.n 6: God's Unusual Speech

1. D. Guthrie and J. A. Motyer, *The New Bible Commentary* (Grand Rapids, MI: Eerdmans, 1991), 97.

2. John Baillie, *A Diary of Private Prayer* (New York: Scribner, 1949), 63.

Conversation 7: Hearing God in the Word

1. William Barclay, 68.
2. Barclay, 67.
3. *Strong's Hebrew and Greek Dictionaries.*
4. John Baillie, *A Diary of Private Prayer* (New York: Scribner, 1949), 63.

About the Author

Jan Johnson is the author of nineteen books, including *Savoring God's Word* and *When the Soul Listens*, and more than a thousand magazine articles and Bible studies. Also a speaker, teacher, and spiritual director, she lives with her husband in Simi Valley, California (www.janjohnson.org). She holds a DMin in Ignatian spirituality and spiritual direction and writes primarily about spiritual formation topics.

Learn from Jan Johnson
how to grow in Christ.

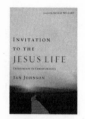

Invitation to the Jesus Life
Jan Johnson

978-1-60006-146-2

Would you like to be drenched with love, focused on others, and filled with courage? Jan Johnson offers a closer look at seventeen underrated qualities of Jesus to help you become more like Jesus. Spiritual practices, as well as questions and group-study suggestions, are included at the end of each chapter.

Living in the Companionship of God
Jan Johnson

978-1-60006-659-7

Get away from it all with God. This unique retreat guide can help direct your thoughts to the underlying needs of your soul. Ideal for one- or three-day personal or group retreats. Includes seven self-contained sessions.

Trusting God for Everything: Psalm 23
Jan Johnson

978-1-60006-661-0

You're packing for a weekend retreat, just to be alone with God. *Trusting God for Everything: Psalm 23* is an outstanding retreat guide to take along to help you grow closer to God. Includes seven self-contained sessions.

To order copies, call NavPress at 1-800-366-7788 or
log on to www.navpress.com.